Volume Four

D1239745

HOW TO PAINT TROPICALS

Volume Four

HOW TO PAINT TROPICALS

Curtis J. Badger

STACKPOLE
BOOKS

Published by
STACKPOLE BOOKS
5067 Ritter Road
Mechanicsburg, PA 17055

Printed in Hong Kong

10 9 8 7 6 5 4 3 2 1

First edition

Cover design by Caroline Miller

Interior design by Marcia Lee Dobbs

Cover photograph by Bob Berry

Library of Congress Cataloging-in-Publication Data

Badger, Curtis J.
    Fish carving basics.

    Contents: v. 1. How to Carve.—v. 2. How to paint.
    1. Wood-carving—Technique. 2. Fishes in art.
    3. Painting—Technique. I. Title.
TT199.7.B335 1994 731'.832   93-30588
ISBN 0-8117-2524-3 (v. 1)
ISBN 0-8117-2440-9 (v. 2)
ISBN 0-8117-2458-1 (v. 3)
ISBN 0-8117-2760-2 (v. 4)

Contents

Foreword

Books such as this are by necessity a team project. First, there are the artists whose work is shown here, a talented group of people whose generosity is equal to their ability with carving tools and paints. Many thanks to Meg Streams of Pennsylvania, Clark Schreibeis of Montana, Rick Roth of Massachusetts, and Bob Swain of Virginia, all of whom unselfishly share their special techniques in this volume of Fish Carving Basics.

Thanks also go to Timothy Effrem and his wife, Deborah, who have supported the art of wood carving in many ways, including sponsorship of the Global Carving Challenge, which Deborah chairs. In addition, they have both worked tirelessly in promoting aquatic life wood carving as an art form. They helped with this series by introducing me to many talented carvers. For more information on the Global Challenge or for a free catalog of carving supplies, contact them at Wood Carvers Supply, Inc., P.O. Box 7500, Englewood, FL 34295-7500, or phone 813-698-0123 or 800-284-6229.

This series would not have been possible without the enthusiastic support of Stackpole Books, and primarily Judith Schnell, the editorial director. So thanks to Judith, the editorial staff, the designers, and all the team members involved in the production aspects of Fish Carving Basics.

Introduction

Tropical fish fascinate us because they are at once beautiful and mysterious. Many are native to exotic parts of the world, yet they are at home in aquariums and can readily be viewed as they go about their daily lives.

These qualities make tropical fish a favorite among carvers. Game fish such as bass and trout are popular because they symbolize outdoor sport; a carving of a jumping bass might remind a fisherman of a particularly thrilling moment in his or her life. But the little tropical fish shown in these demonstrations are not game fish—the cherubfish carved by Bob Swain is only 2½ inches long—and they capture the imagination of the artists simply because of their exotic beauty.

The intent of this book, and indeed of the entire Fish Carving Basics series, is to demonstrate that there are many ways to approach the art. Art is a very personal endeavor, and so are the techniques one employs to reach a desired end. The techniques demonstrated in this book are personal and varied, and they are included here not for you to copy, but to tweak your imagination and encourage you to develop a style and approach all your own. In art, there is no right way or wrong way of doing things. There is instead a vast menu of options awaiting your choice.

The techniques shown here range from highly realistic fish depicted in an equally realistic setting, to folk art fish that are simple in design and rendered with a minimum of detail. Rick Roth is one of the world's best at the former technique, and Bob Swain is a master of the latter.

In this book, Rick paints a French angelfish, which he mounts in a coral setting that includes a moray eel. Bob carves and paints a school of four cherubfish. Rick uses modern high-speed cutting tools and electric burning pens, and he paints the fish with an airbrush. Bob carves his fish with a knife and wood rasp, and he paints it with a brush and sign paint, and then sets the paint on fire.

Although the techniques of these two artists are miles apart, both are very valid and are the means to the end envisioned by the artist. As I said, art is a personal matter, and so are the techniques one may use. Technique, after all, is simply a way of creating a tangible form based on an image you create in your mind. Your job as a carver is to determine what technique best transforms that mental image into a tangible one.

Rick Roth is a master of the airbrush; Bob Swain is an accomplished contemporary folk artist; and Meg Streams is a talented painter who eschews the airbrush for acrylic tube paints. And thus we have a third option for you, painting fish with brushes. Meg owns an airbrush, but she prefers the control and quietness of painting with brushes. The two demonstrations herein confirm her outstanding ability to do so.

If you are new to the field of fish carving, perhaps tube paints and brushes would be a good place to start. Airbrushes, after all, represent a considerable investment. Meg's demonstration of painting the long-nosed butterfly fish is especially recommended for beginners. Though the fish is strikingly beautiful, the palette of colors required is modest, and no special techniques are needed.

To round out this volume of Fish Carving Basics, we have two brief demonstrations. One is on carving and bending fins by Meg, and the other is on making a plastic cast of a fish. The latter is by Clark Schreibeis of Billings, Montana, whose work is featured in *Fish Carving Basics: How to Paint Trout.*

I hope you enjoy seeing how these talented artists go about their work, and I hope you will be inspired to develop carving and painting techniques all your own.

1

Painting a Queen Angelfish with Margaret Streams

Can an affinity for wood carving be passed along by genetic code? In the case of Meg Streams of Lederach, Pennsylvania, evidence points in that direction. Her father, Dr. William Sugden, is an accomplished bird carver whose work is included in the collection of the prestigious Ward Museum in Salisbury, Maryland. Meg grew up amid an atmosphere of wildlife and wood chips.

"My father has carved birds for as long as I can remember," she says. "Our family vacations were scheduled around the Ward shows. So I learned the right carving techniques, how to use a burning tool, how to paint."

Meg began her own carving career in 1990 when she temporarily moved in with her parents after a divorce. "I moved into the basement and started using my dad's tools," she says. "My first bird was an avocet, which I still have, and then I did a wood duck and a ruddy duck. I was frustrated because my work wasn't as good as my father's. I didn't think it measured up."

So Meg set out to discover her own approach to the art, and she found it when attending a carving show with her aunt. "I saw Bob Berry's book on fish carving [*Carving Freshwater Fish*] and became very interested," she says. "I bought the book and carved my first fish."

Still, it has taken a while for Meg to develop her own style and technique. "My first fish was kind of square and had bulging eyes," she says. "I thought it was awful, but my parents loved it and they still have it displayed in the family room."

In the past few years, Meg's career has blossomed. She joined a local carving club, Wilhelm Schimmel Carvers in Quakertown, Pennsylvania, and won a first place in club competition with the first bluegill she had ever carved. "Competing sparked my interest, and I saw an ad for the Global Carving Challenge, which at that time was held in Norfolk, Virginia," Meg recalls. "I entered and met Tim and Debbie Effrem, who sponsor the event, and Howard Suzuki and Mark Frazier, who were judges. They've been my mentors. I took seminars with them, and after the judging they would critique my work. It's been very valuable."

A wall in Meg's studio attests to her successes in the Global competition. In 1994 she won first and second places in the saltwater fish category with a queen angelfish and a red-headed butterfly fish, respectively. She also took a second in freshwater fish with a trio of goldfish. In 1993 she won a second in saltwater for a pair of long-nosed butterfly fish. A lionfish won second in saltwater in 1992.

Meg recently married Dale Streams, a veterinarian, and they are planning a new home with a large shop and studio, complete with a saltwater aquarium, the ultimate in reference material for a fish carver.

Prior to painting, Meg uses a pyrographic instrument to burn-in the scales. She uses a C-shaped tip on the pen, which makes it easy to create the illusion of overlapping scales. She uses gouges to carve the fins and adds fine detail with the burning pen. Super Glue is applied to the fins to add strength, and a spray sanding sealer is used before painting.

After learning carving techniques from her father and taking seminars with other artists, Meg is confident in her own style and approach to carving. She prefers hand tools to power tools and prefers brushes and acrylic paints to an airbrush, although she does use one on occasion. "With some of my winnings at the Global show I got a high-speed grinder and a lot of diamond bits, but I rarely use it," she says. "I like chip carving and I'm stuck in my ways. I carve to relax, and I don't like the dust and noise of the power tools and the air compressor."

In this demonstration Meg paints a queen angelfish, using brushes and acrylic paints. The fish was carved from basswood, which Meg says works well with a knife.

Paints used in this demonstration include thio violet, endo orange red, cadmium orange, ivory black, chromium oxide green, dioxazine purple, ultramarine blue, cerulean blue, neutral gray, raw sienna, and cadmium yellow deep. All are Liquitex, except for the thio violet, ultramarine blue, and cadmium yellow, which are Grumbacher.

For information on Meg Streams's carvings, contact her at Quakertown Vet Clinic, 2250 Old Bethlehem Pike, Quakertown, PA 18951.

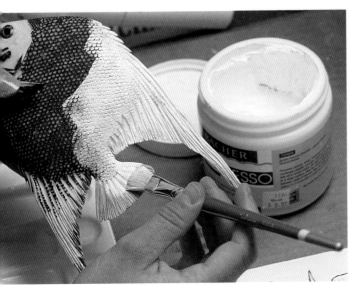

The base coat is a 2:1 mixture of titanium white and gesso diluted with water. The base coat should be applied in several thin washes; a heavy application could obscure carved detail. Meg will apply three coats here, allowing each to dry before recoating.

The first color to be applied is Liquitex cadmium yellow deep, which goes on the fins and the area around the eye. Yellow extends from the fin onto the caudal peduncle.

Meg uses two coats of yellow, drying the paint with a blow dryer between applications. The area of yellow on the face varies in shape from fish to fish. Meg uses photographs as reference material.

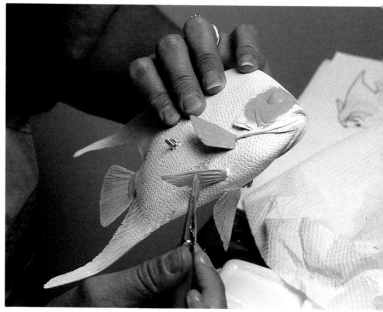

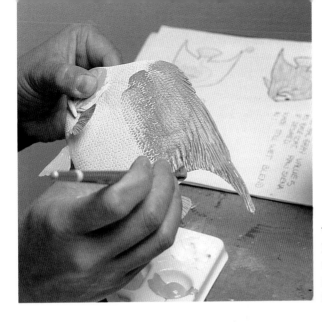

With the fins and face painted, Meg puts on a base coat of neutral gray, to which is added a small amount of raw sienna to make it slightly brown.

The gray-brown coat will serve as a base color and is applied to the entire fish, except the areas that have been painted yellow.

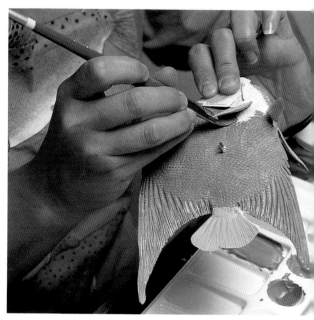

The gray-brown wash should be fairly thin. "It doesn't have to cover completely," Meg says, "but be sure to scrub it into the scales so it will cover the white gesso in the carved detail. If you get paint on the fins, cover it with yellow."

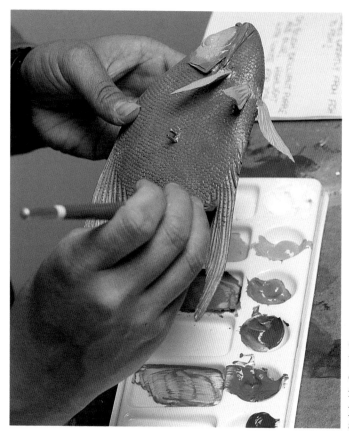

Cerulean blue goes on the belly and lower chin, and on the face and maxillaries. Again, the paint is applied in thin washes, and several coats are put on.

A mixture of ultramarine blue and dioxazene purple is applied to the sides of the fish. "You apply the paint wet-on-wet and blend the areas where they meet," says Meg. "The first couple of coats will look awful, but don't despair."

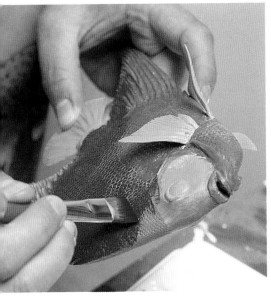

"At this stage, application of color is not exact," says Meg. "The cerulean blue and blue/purple areas overlap. If you get paint on the yellow, you can cover it later. The dorsal fin is not painted at this point."

This shows the gradations in color, from violet on the back to ultramarine blue on the sides and cerulean blue on the belly. The margins are not exact, so don't worry about being too precise, Meg advises.

The next color to be applied is chromium oxide green, which goes on the trailing edge of the dorsal fin, the anal fin, and the upper back and head.

Again, Meg applies the paint in a wet-to-wet technique, blending the edges where the colors meet

While the purple is wet, Meg applies more blue and blends those colors together. The idea is to create a soft edge between them and to have one overlapping the other.

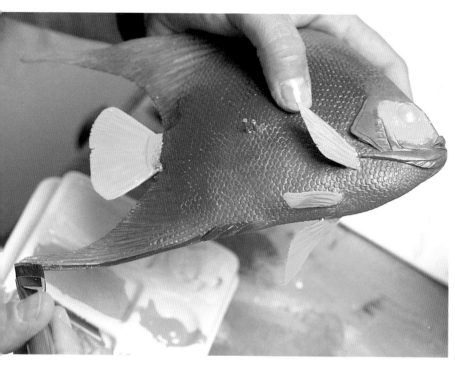

A purple stripe is painted on the leading edge of the anal fin. Meg uses straight dioxyzene purple.

Purple also is used to edge the green dorsal fin, going on both the leading and trailing edges.

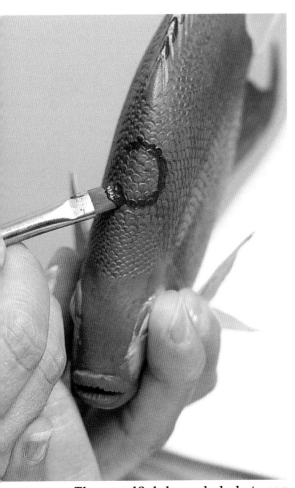

The angelfish has a halo between the head and the dorsal fin. Meg adds this detail by first painting a circle with dioxazine purple.

A small amount of cerulean blue is used to highlight the purple halo.

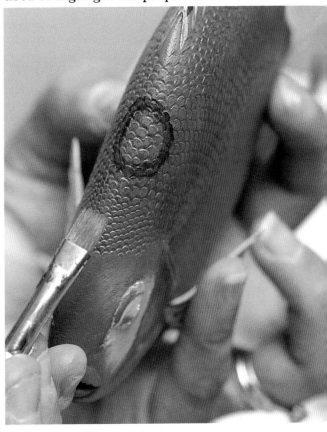

Cerulean blue is lightened with titanium white and is used to create highlights on the extreme edges of the dorsal fin. These marks vary from fish to fish, so pay attention to your reference material.

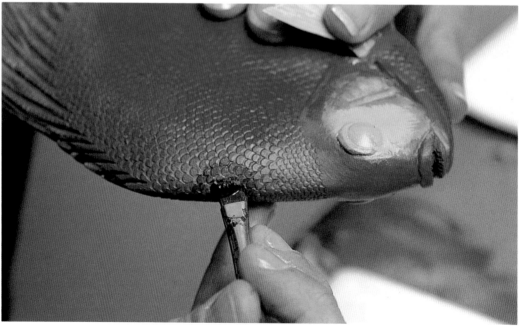

The center of the halo is black, and Meg paints this using ivory black straight from the tube.

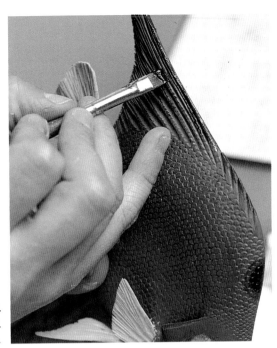

Ivory black is also used to paint a thin line inside the purple edge on the dorsal fin.

The black band widens on the trailing edge of the dorsal fin where it nears the caudal fin.

Black is used on the inside of the purple line on the anal fin. Meg also will use it to paint a circle at the base of both pectoral fins.

Cerulean blue is used to tip each scale on the outer edges of the halo. This step adds highlights and depth.

Cerulean blue goes in the circles in front of the pectoral fins. A small amount of ultramarine blue is added to cerulean blue, and this is used to paint triangular markings on the sides of the face.

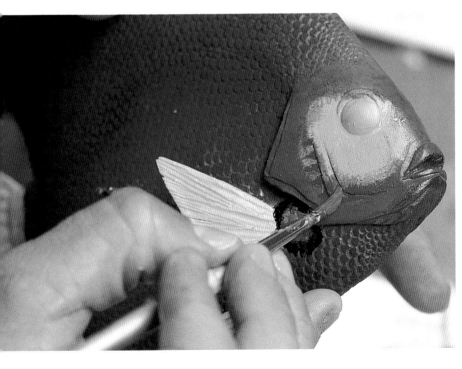

The same blue is used to highlight detail on the face. Here it is applied to the edges of the gill covers.

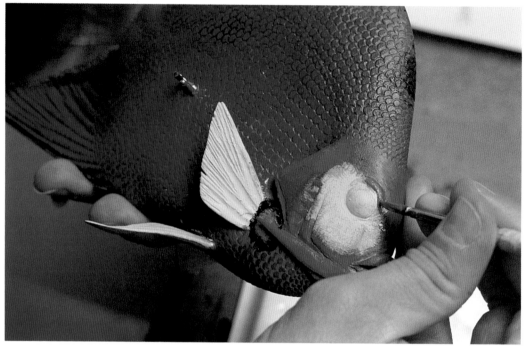

The face of the angelfish often has blue splotches, which Meg adds during this step. Here she paints the eyelid.

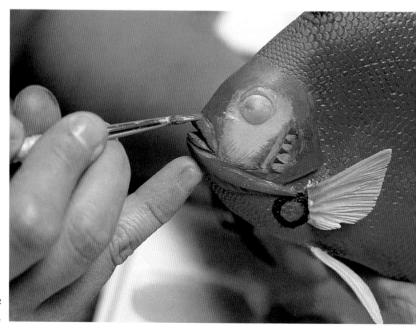

The lips of the fish are painted blue.

Ivory black is used to tip the scales on the caudal peduncle. On the angelfish, Meg dabs black on the center of each scale. With some fish, such as trout, the color is applied to the trailing edge.

Meg is now ready to paint the dorsal and anal fins, using a combination of cadmium orange, endo red orange, and thio violet. She will use a dry-brushing technique, scrubbing the paint into the texture of the carving.

She combines the two orange colors, then adds a small amount of violet to create a magenta color. The brush is fairly dry, and she lightly touches the paint onto the spiny rays of the dorsal fin.

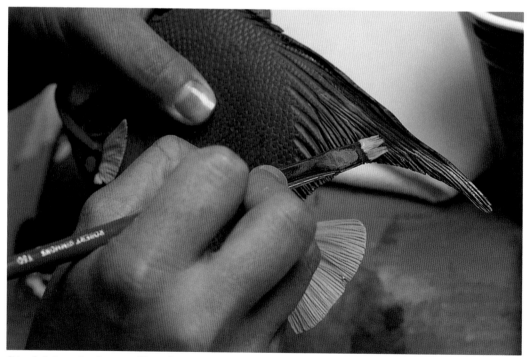

Straight cadmium yellow is used as a highlight in some areas. Again, the brush is nearly dry and just a small amount of color is added.

The paint job is nearly complete, but before Meg begins scale-tipping she will add a nearly transparent coat of Polytranspar shimmering blue to the green, purple, and blue areas. This will add a small amount of reflectance.

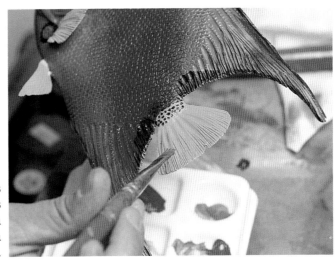

A very weak wash of green is painted over the caudal fin. This settles into the grooves between the rays and provides definition and depth.

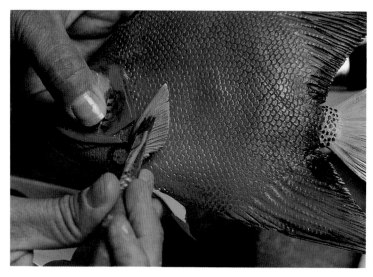

The same wash is used on the pectoral fins. The color should be weak, just enough to avoid having a solid yellow color.

A final step is to mix small amounts of green, brown, and black and brush it lightly across the rays of the caudal fin. This darkens the edges of the rays and adds more definition. The brush should be nearly dry.

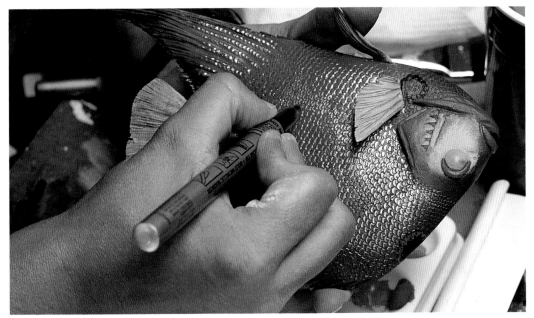

Meg scale-tips the angelfish with a Sanford gold metallic marking pen purchased from an office supply store. She tips the trailing edge of each scale. The reflective gold adds a realistic shimmer to the fish, which will change color as the direction of the light striking it changes.

Paint is scraped from the eye with a scalpel blade.

The angelfish has been scale-tipped and is ready to be sprayed with an acrylic clear coat. Meg warns that if you use a marking pen you should test it first to make sure it is compatible with your paints and with any clear spray finish you may use.

The angelfish is finished and mounted on a branch of coral. A second fish will be added later to the composition.

2
Painting a Long-nosed Butterfly Fish with Margaret Streams

The long-nosed butterfly fish is a perfect project for beginning carvers, says Meg Streams, who presents a painting demonstration in this chapter. With its long nose and broad fins, it's a striking looking fish, yet the painting process is relatively simple and requires no special techniques and a limited palette of colors.

The long-nosed butterfly fish (*Forcipiger flavissimus*) is a widespread saltwater tropical fish, living in the Indo-Pacific from the Red Sea and the coast of East Africa to Easter Island, Hawaii, and the coast of Mexico. Its brilliant color and unusual shape make it a popular aquarium fish, as well as a favorite for fish carvers.

Meg will paint the fish with water-soluble acrylic colors, first applying a coat of white gesso to provide a uniform painting surface. Her palette for this project includes cerulean blue, ivory black, raw umber, iridescent white, titanium white, and three values of yellow: cadmium yellow medium, cadmium deep, and Turner's yellow.

She uses four brushes: a half-inch round sable Grumbacher brush for painting broad areas and applying gesso, a size 8 Grumbacher, a size 2 Grumbacher, and a small tipping brush for fine detail.

"It's an easy fish to paint because the color of the body varies a great deal from fish to fish," she says. "So the painter has a lot of leeway. If you look at photos in books, you'll find everything from whitish yellow on the belly and sides to a solid, deep yellow."

Meg adds that this fish is a good project for beginners or those on a limited budget because it can be painted with just a few colors. "You can buy a tube of yellow, one of white, one of brown, and borrow a little blue from somebody, and that's all you really need," she says.

The rather spectacular coloration of the fish is a defense mechanism, a means of confusing predators. "It has a dark triangle that splits the eye, and there is a false eye spot near the tail, so a predator would have a hard time telling which is the head and which is the tail," says Meg. "And the tail is a dark, smoky color, which is nearly invisible under water. So a potential predator does not see a fish shape when it spots a long-nosed butterfly fish. This is a striking fish to the human eye, but its beauty serves a purpose."

The fish, which is carved from basswood, has been textured with a pyrographic instrument to replicate scales and fin rays, and the wood has been sealed with acrylic clearcoat. Before painting, Meg applies one or more coats of white gesso diluted fifty-fifty with water.

The gesso is worked into the texture of the fish, covering the charred wood. Meg uses a large brush and works the medium into the scales and fins.

White gesso provides a uniform painting surface, which is especially important when using light colors, such as yellow. If a fish were primarily dark, the gesso could be darkened by adding black acrylic paint.

The goal when applying gesso is to get a uniform surface, without splotches, but not to obscure the finely carved detail. Diluting the gesso with water helps in this regard.

Meg dries the gesso with a hair dryer, and then applies a small amount of iridescent white to the lower jaw, the muscle in front of the pectoral fin, and the gill plates, which will be white in the finished fish.

Meg is ready to apply the yellow, and to do so she mixes three values of yellow—cadmium medium, cadmium deep, and Turner's—until she has a color she's happy with. The three colors on her palette are, from the top, cadmium medium, Turner's, and cadmium deep. On the left are gesso and iridescent white.

"I mix the three and just see how the color turns out," she says. "I probably use equal amounts of each. When I want to lighten the yellow I add a little titanium white."

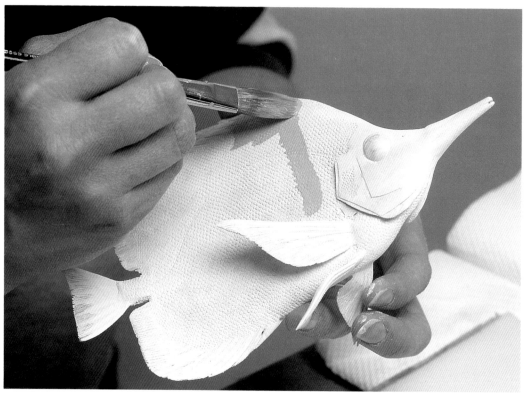

Meg begins painting on the front portion of the body, behind the dorsal fin where the yellow will meet the dark triangle that will cover the fish's head.

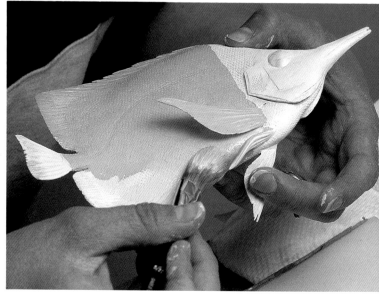

She wants the belly of the fish and the anal fin to be a lighter value of yellow, so she adds a small amount of titanium white to the yellow and blends the two colors together while they are wet, creating a smooth transition.

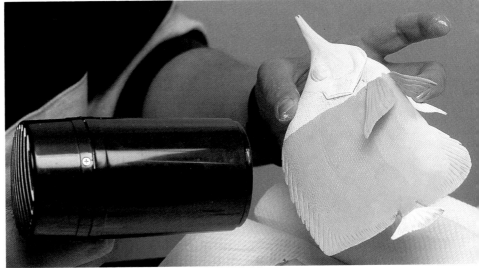

A small hair dryer comes in handy when drying the paint, thus reducing the amount of time between coats.

Raw umber is used to paint the dark triangle that covers the top of the head. Meg uses it straight from the tube, mixing the paint with a little water.

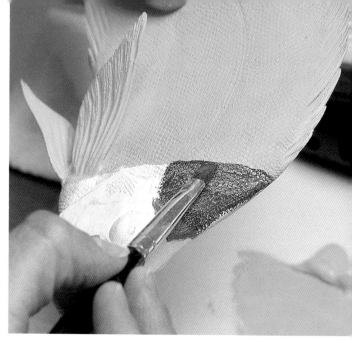

The brown cap meets the yellow of the body, creating a hard edge that will be softened later.

The raw umber goes midway through the eye. The brown area is not a solid color and should be applied somewhat unevenly. Meg uses the smaller brush here and blots on the color.

Raw umber is applied through the eyeline and along the top of the nose. Photographs from various books and guides are used as reference material when determining the color and the placement of the markings.

Meg squeezes most of the paint from the brush and blots a few raw umber marks on the gill plates of the fish. These should be splotchy and random, and the dry-brush technique works well for this.

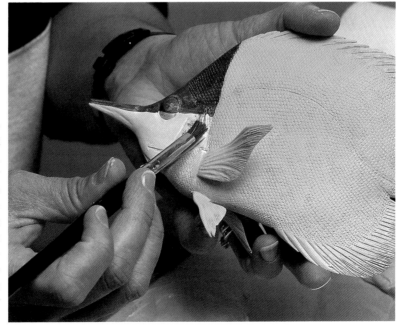

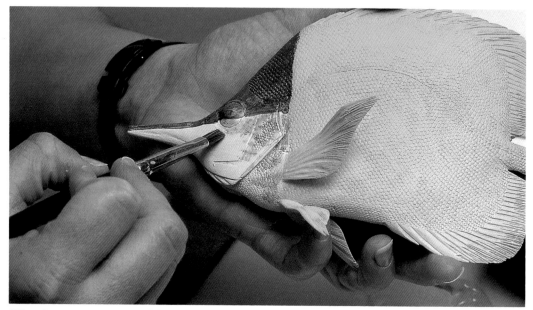

"You just want to muddy it up a little, to cover the white on the gill plates and in front of the pectoral fins," says Meg. "There are no hard and fast rules. Every fish I've seen is a little bit different, so don't worry about making mistakes."

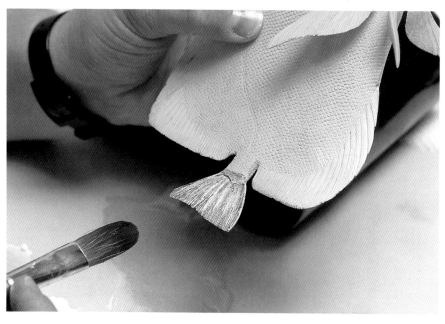

The raw umber paint is also used to darken the tail fin, to create that smoky look. Meg adds a small amount of ivory black to darken and slightly cool the value of the raw umber.

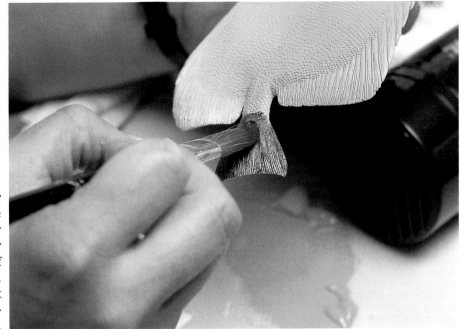

The brown color extends into the yellow body color. Two or more washes of paint are used, with each coat dried before another is applied.

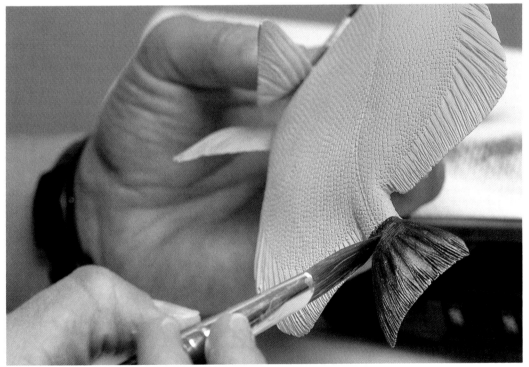

The brown should be darker at the base of the tail fin, so an additional wash goes here.

The pectoral fins are transparent on a live long-nosed butterfly fish, a look that is difficult to replicate using wood and paint. Meg uses the dry-brush technique to add just a little of the raw umber mix to the tops of the spiny rays.

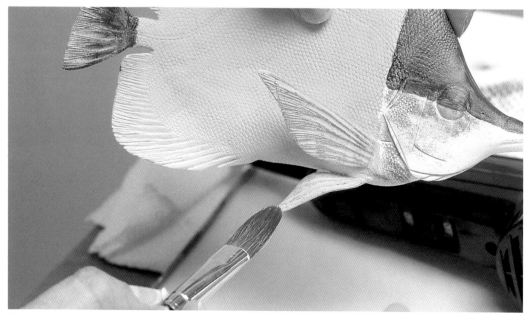

The raw umber mix is applied to both sides of the fins. "You just want to darken the fins a bit, to help make the spines show up," says Meg.

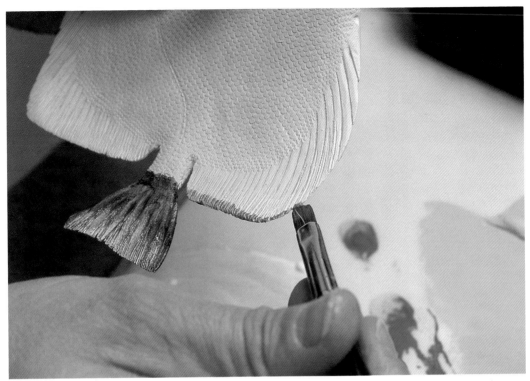

There is a thin blue line on the trailing edges of
the anal and dorsal fins. Meg adds this by applying
cerulean blue diluted with water using the size 8
brush.

A second wash is applied,
darkening the blue notice-
ably. It often will take two
or more coats to cover the
yellow. An alternative
would be to leave the edge
unpainted when the yel-
low is applied, and paint
the blue directly onto the
white gesso.

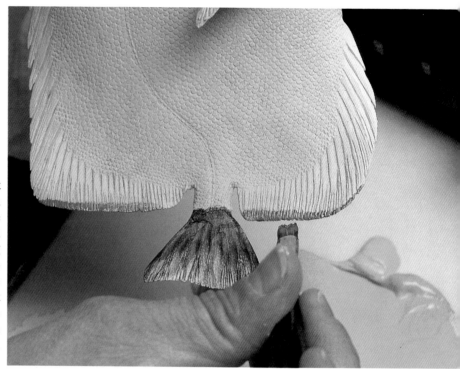

Be sure to paint the blue line on both sides of the anal and dorsal fins. Here Meg adds the line to the reverse side of the fin just painted. The blue line will be highlighted with white later.

With the blue paint on her palette, Meg will add a little to the lower jaw and chest of the fish. She uses the large brush, adding a bit of iridescent white to lighten the blue.

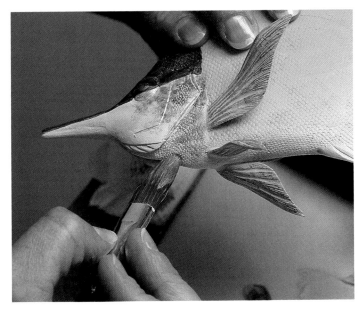

These fish vary in the amount of blue in this area, so it's up to the painter to determine how much blue to add. Blue adds a translucent quality to gill plates and scales.

Meg adds a little more iridescent white to the gill plates. If you get too much blue paint here, lighten it with iridescent white.

The eye spot goes on the anal fin, just below the tail. Meg uses ivory black straight from the tube and applies it with a size 2 brush.

Next, white highlights are added to the blue line on the dorsal and anal fins. Titanium white is applied with a very small tipping brush.

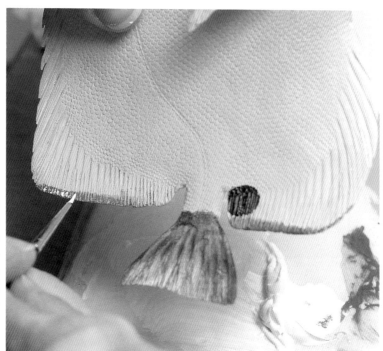

Titanium white is used with a dry-brush technique to add subtle highlights to the spiny rays on the fins. Meg blots most of the paint from the brush and drags it across the tops of the rays.

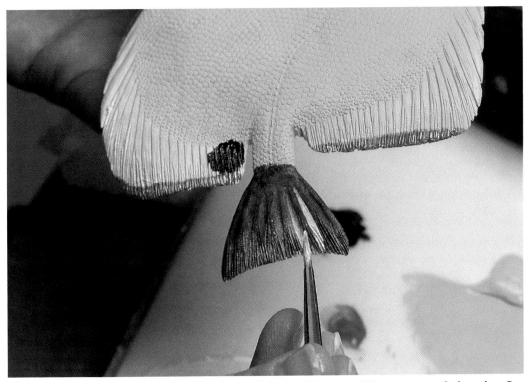

Titanium white is diluted with water, and the size 2 brush is used to add detail to the tail fin. In this step, the paint is applied in the troughs between the rays.

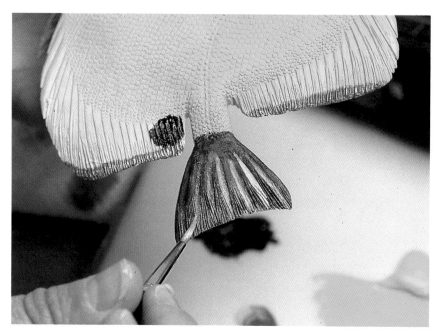

These white lines are not necessarily on the live fish, but they help lend a smoky, translucent look to a wooden fin.

Meg uses the large brush to touch up the line separating the yellow body and the brown of the cap. The brush has an uneven edge, and this helps create a slightly ragged margin between the two colors. As a final touch-up, Meg adds a thin wash of raw umber over the head. This makes the brown splotches dabbed on earlier a little more subtle. The fish is dried with the hair dryer, and now all that remains is the removal of paint from the eyes and an application of clear sealer. A scalpel blade is used to remove paint from the eyes. Meg scores the paint around the edges, then gently lifts it off with the blade. Krylon Crystal Clear acrylic coating is used to seal the fish. The spray protects the paint and adds a slight gloss.

40

3 Carving Fins for a Veil-tailed Goldfish with Margaret Streams

Two years ago Meg carved an entry for the Global Carving Challenge depicting a trio of veil-tailed goldfish, whose caudal fins are very thin and wavy. Faced with the challenge of depicting those waves in wood, she adopted a method of woodworking long a tradition in the boatbuilding business.

Using very thin basswood sheets, she cuts out the pattern with the grain running horizontally. Using a small gouge, she scores the fin on both sides, using pen marks to align the gouge tracks. She sandpapers the wood to smooth it and eliminate sharp edges. Then a V-gouge is used to define individual rays on both sides. Finally, she cleans up the gouge marks with a burning tool.

When the carving is completed, the fin is extremely thin and will flex. Meg places it into a pot of hot water for about five minutes and then bends it around a glass or can, using rubber bands and various size paintbrushes to create irregular waves. The fin dries overnight, and then is removed and strengthened with an application of Super Glue.

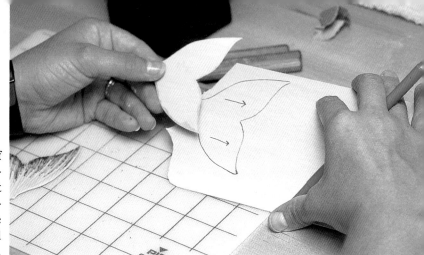

The fin is cut out of a thin sheet of basswood, available at carving supply dealers. Grain runs in the direction indicated by the arrows.

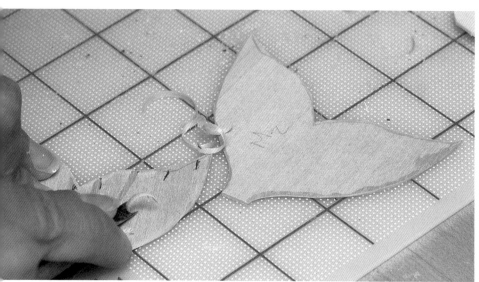

A small gouge is used to score the fin on both sides. Pen marks help align the gouge tracks.

Gouge marks divide the fin into approximately ten sections. The wood is very thin where the gouge tracks are back-to-back.

Fine sandpaper is
used to smooth the edges.

Individual spines are carved
with a micro V-gouge, and these are
cleaned with a burning pen.

The fin is placed in hot water for
about five minutes, then
wrapped around a can or glass,
with paintbrush handles used to
incorporate bends and folds.

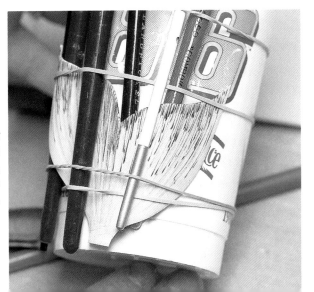

The dried caudal fin has a very realistic wavy look.

An application of Super Glue strengthens the fin.

The fin is applied to the goldfish.

4 Making a Cast of a Tinker's Butterfly Fish with Clark Schreibeis

One of the best items of reference material in the carver's arsenal is a cast made from a fresh fish. A cast is not difficult to make, the materials are readily available, and it's the next best thing to having a live fish on hand when you need to check on a subtle detail of fish anatomy.

In this demonstration, Clark Schreibeis of Billings, Montana, makes a cast of a tinker's butterfly fish. He makes a mold with dental alginate, the material used by dentists to take impressions of teeth, and then fills the mold with automobile body filler to make the casting. Dental alginate is available at dental supply businesses or from taxidermy suppliers.

Clark begins by making a cardboard enclosure to hold the alginate. The enclosure is then filled to about half its depth, and the fish is pressed into the material while it is still wet. When the alginate sets, Clark adds a second application, covering the top of the fish. When the top layer is set, he separates the two halves, removes the fish, and fills the cavity with body filler. The filler hardens in about ten minutes, producing a highly detailed impression of the butterfly fish.

For information on Clark Schreibeis's carvings, contact him at 5626 Danford Road, Billings, MT 59106.

Clark begins by making a cardboard enclosure that
will hold the dental alginate. The enclosure should
be slightly larger than the fish and should be deep
enough to provide at least an inch thickness for
each side of the mold.

Dental alginate,
a powder, is
mixed with wa-
ter to make a
paste, which is
poured into the
cardboard en-
closure. The
fish is then
pressed into the
material.

The alginate will set up in three or four minutes. When it does, Clark uses a knife to cut several holes in the bottom half of the mold. These will fill with alginate when the top half is poured and will serve as keys to keep the two halves in register when the cast is made.

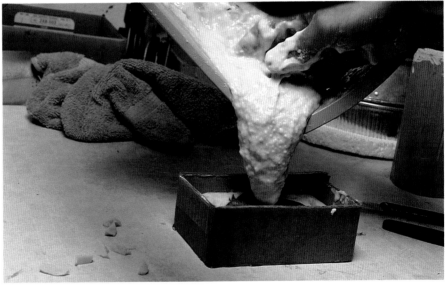

With the bottom half set, Clark pours alginate to form the top half of the mold. Because the bottom half is set, it will not adhere to the liquid alginate being poured.

In a few minutes the alginate sets up and becomes rubbery. Clark removes the cardboard enclosure.

The two halves are carefully pulled apart, and the fish is removed.

Alginate is capable of recording extremely fine detail and is particularly useful for documenting fin detail, scale shape, and fine details around the mouth and head. Note the keyholes Clark cut in the mold; these will ensure that the two halves are in register when the cast is made.

Auto body filler is mixed according to package directions and is brushed into both halves of the alginate mold. It's necessary to work quickly because the body filler will harden in a few minutes.

Clark presses the two halves of the mold together, then lets the body filler harden.

After about fifteen minutes, the two halves of the mold are carefully pulled apart. The mold is fragile and not permanent, but Clark could use it to make one or two more casts if he wanted to.

With the mold separated, the cast butterfly fish appears. Note the fine detail captured in the fins and the head.

The three-dimensional cast is complete and will be added to Clark's file of reference material. He was beginning a commission piece depicting a tinker's butterfly fish when this demonstration was done, and the cast fish will be invaluable as he begins the carving process.

5

Painting a French Angelfish with Rick Roth

Rick Roth of Littleton, Massachusetts, is a master of the airbrush. He demonstrated his technique on a brown trout in *Fish Carving Basics: How to Paint Trout*, and in this volume on tropical fish he paints a French angelfish, a colorful fish of the Caribbean that sometimes can be found along the coast of North America.

Rick was in the aquarium business before taking up carving, and he often made collecting trips to Florida and the Caribbean islands for fish such as the French angel. Today, however, Rick's concerns are with conserving and carving fish, not capturing them for aquariums. His work is in galleries around the country, and he is represented by Wildlife Reflections of Fitchburg, Massachusetts.

Rick, with Bob Blain of Wildlife Reflections, recently began a conservation program called Catch and Release Carvings, in which he carves trophy fish for anglers who release their catch alive. Anglers measure and photograph their fish and send the data to Rick, and he carves them a replica for display. The cost, he says, is comparable to good-quality taxidermy. The buyer gets not only a trophy to mark an outstanding catch, but also a work of wildlife art. And the fish, of course, gets to swim away.

In this demonstration Rick paints a French angelfish that is mature but still bears a bit of the striped parr markings of youth. These fish vary widely in coloration according to age and environment, and Rick paints this fish based on information gathered from reference photos. He does not use a color schedule be-

51

cause French angels vary so much in color. Instead, he uses photographs of live fish as a guide.

The fish is carved from tupelo and will be mounted on a maple base that includes several varieties of coral and a moray eel. Rick will paint the fish with Wasco Polytranspar taxidermy paints applied with an airbrush. As the demonstration begins, Rick has primed the surface with gesso, which is brushed on in several diluted applications to avoid obscuring finely carved detail. Any gesso that gets on the eyes is scraped off before painting.

The fish is striking, but the colors required are few. "It's a fairly easy fish to paint," says Rick. "You don't need that many colors, but with all the yellow the fish is really stunning looking."

Rick uses base colors of phthalo blue on the head and Payne's gray and black umber on the body. Yellow is used to accent the dorsal and anal fins, and the scales are outlined with yellow acrylic paint applied with a size 3 brush.

For information on Rick Roth's carving and painting seminars, contact him at 132 Nashoba Road, Littleton, MA 01460. For information on Catch and Release Carvings and other works by Rick, contact Wildlife Reflections, P.O. Box 2261, Fitchburg, MA 01420.

Rick applies several thin coats of gesso with a bristle brush to provide a uniform painting surface, and after it has dried he begins adding color with the airbrush. Wasco Polytranspar phthalo blue is applied to the head of the fish.

The color is built up gradually until it reaches the value Rick wants. The paint is applied to the gill covers, the head, and the face. Rick isn't concerned about overspray now because the edges of the blue will be blended into the darker body color later, and any overspray will be covered.

Photographs of French angelfish are kept on Rick's workbench as he paints, and he refers to them often. Instead of using a color schedule, he depends upon photos because fish vary in color depending upon age and environment.

The application of blue is complete, and now Rick is ready to apply the body color, Polytranspar Payne's gray. A fine mist of Payne's gray will be added to the head to subdue the blue somewhat.

Rick begins by applying Payne's gray to the dorsal fin. "Payne's gray is a cool, slightly bluish value of gray, and the color changes somewhat from brand to brand," says Rick. If the color is too cool and bluish, a final misting of black umber will warm it.

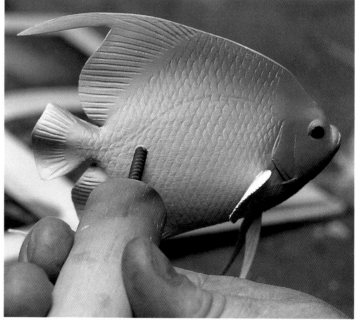

When Rick sprays Payne's gray, a dark color, he dilutes the paint slightly with Polytranspar clearcoat medium and a few drops of water. This produces a lighter value and gives Rick more control so that he can build the color up gradually.

The dorsal, anal, pectoral, and pelvic fins are all painted with Payne's gray. Yellow will later be applied to the dorsal and anal fins, but rather than trying to mask those areas, Rick paints them now and will later reprime them with white before adding yellow.

In comparing the color of the fish with reference photos, Rick decides that the Payne's gray is too blue, so he adds a light application of black umber to warm it. "Polytranspar black umber is a combination of chocolate and black, and is handy for warming up cool grays," Rick says.

It's easy to forget to paint behind the pectoral fins, and painting them is difficult once the fish has been detailed. Rick makes sure to paint them at this stage. He also makes sure that the paint is applied symmetrically and is the same on both sides. "Painting in front of a mirror could help with this, in that you see both sides of the fish at the same time," Rick says.

At this stage, the phthalo blue has been applied to the head and has been blended into the Payne's gray body color. The gray was used to darken the blue slightly, and then black umber was used to warm up the coolish Payne's gray. These comprise the base colors of the angelfish. Now Rick is ready to add detail.

This particular fish Rick is painting is mature, but it still shows some of the parr markings, or vertical striping, of its youth. Rick will add them by spraying Polytranspar Superhide white.

One fairly wide stripe begins at the top of the dorsal fin and extends downward across the body just behind the pectoral fin. A smaller and less distinct stripe begins just behind the head and extends behind the eyes. Again, make sure paint is applied in the same manner on both sides of the fish.

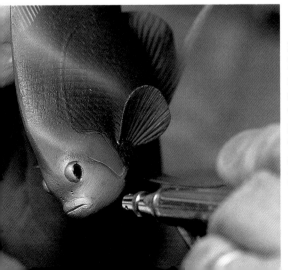

Rick changes to a finer needle in the airbrush as he begins adding fine detail. The mouth of the angelfish is painted white, and while Rick has the airbrush loaded with white, he also paints the dorsal and anal fins in preparation for a later application of yellow. A small dot of yellow is also at the base of the pectoral fins, and Rick paints this white.

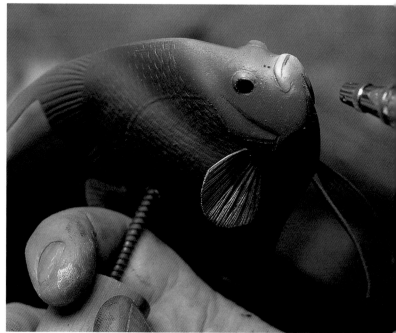

White goes on the chin, and its lower edge is feathered as it meets the blue. An advantage of the airbrush, Rick says, is that it makes it easy to create such soft edges and gradual transitions.

The face of the French angelfish is nearly done. Note the detail around the mouth and eyes and the transition between blue and gray.

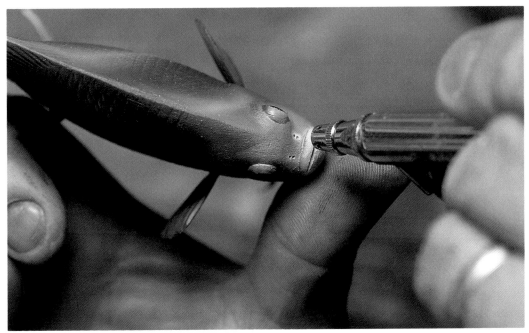

A final step is to paint the nostrils white.

Cadmium yellow is applied to the tip of an anal fin, covering the area painted white in a previous step.

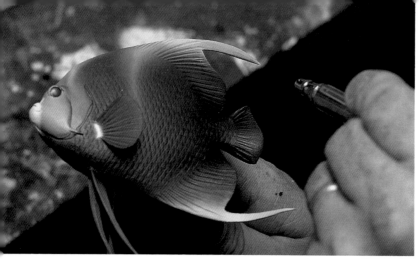

Cadmium yellow is also sprayed on the tips of the dorsal fin. Note how the yellow gradually fades into white where the tip joins the main part of the fin.

A small dab of yellow goes at the base of the two pectoral fins.

On the French angelfish, each scale is outlined in yellow, and Rick does this with a brush and Jo Sonja acrylic paint rather than the airbrush. He uses yellow light and adds a bit of warm white to gain opacity. Tube paints have thicker consistency than airbrush paint and are easier to apply with a brush.

The technique Rick uses is similar to scale-tipping (see *Fish Carving Basics: How to Paint Trout*). A thin line is painted along the edge of each scale. This is a time-consuming step, but an important one.

Rick has almost completed the scales. If the effect is too bold, he can soften it by using the airbrush to spray on a light mist of the body color.

In addition to the scale lines, the French angelfish also has small dots on the dorsal and anal fins. Rick consults his reference photos to determine the size, density, and location of the spots.

The spots on the dorsal and anal fins are in a fairly uniform line following the contour of the body. They are larger near the body of the fish and become smaller toward the edges of the fins.

The membranes covering the eyes are painted yellow. Any paint that spills onto the glass eyes can be scraped off when it dries.

With the paint job completed, Rick sprays on Polytranspar water-based clearcoat to seal the surface and give it a slight gloss. He applies one quick flash coat, allows it to dry, and then sprays on another coat.

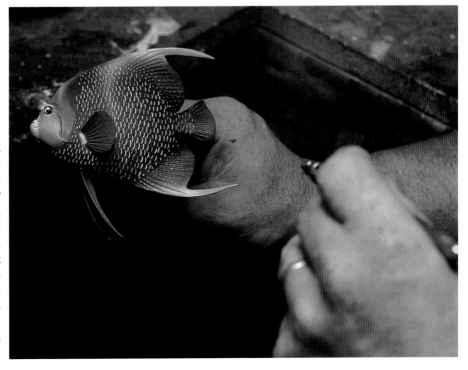

The completed French angelfish is mounted in a setting that includes several types of coral and a moray eel. The base is carved from a maple burl.

Rick at work in his Massachusetts studio.

6
Carving and Painting a School of Cherubfish with Bob Swain

Bob Swain, who lives near the Chesapeake Bay on the Eastern Shore of Virginia, carves fish, birds, and other animals in a style that might be called contemporary folk art. His pieces are carved with hand tools from white pine or cedar, and the designs are simple and graceful.

He paints with Ronan brand oil paints, which are highly saturated colors used mainly in the sign industry. An unusual twist is that Bob burns the paint while it is still wet, a technique that instantly adds a patina of age. An enthusiastic buffing with burlap or a bristle brush further distresses the paint, adding to the illusion of wear and tear.

Burning a carving to add the illusion of age is dangerous, and we recommend less hazardous methods, such as soaking in vinegar or salt water or simply leaving the workpiece outdoors for an appropriate period.

In this demonstration, Bob will carve and paint a school of four cherubfish. The fish are carved from white pine, and once Bob cuts out the blanks on the band saw, all the work is done with hand tools. The fish are carved with knives, then rounded off with a rasp, and finally smoothed with sandpaper.

The four fish are arranged in something of a C-curve composition, which is much more interesting visually than having them on the same vertical plane. Once the fish are carved, Bob arranges them the way he wants them, and then attaches them to each other with small wooden dowels. When the composition is complete, Bob disassembles it to paint each fish separately, then puts it back together when the paint has dried. It usually is necessary to touch up the paint where the dowels connect the fish.

The four cherubfish are mounted on a piece of weathered driftwood using a slender metal rod.

For information on Bob Swain's carvings, contact him at P.O. Box 1631, Parksley, VA 23421.

Bob begins the project by tracing the pattern of the cherubfish onto a piece of white pine approximately ½-inch thick. He made the pattern by sketching the outline of the fish onto cardboard, using photographs as reference. The blank is cut out on a band saw, and the location of the fins is drawn on both sides.

The centerline is drawn around the perimeter of the fish. This line will be left during the carving process, ensuring that the fish will be carved in the proper shape and be symmetrical.

Bob begins carving using a small knife to round out the shape of the fish. "Cherubfish are small—about 2½ inches long—and are difficult to carve with a knife because of their size," Bob says. Carvers who use rotary cutting tools, such as Foredoms, would find the process easier.

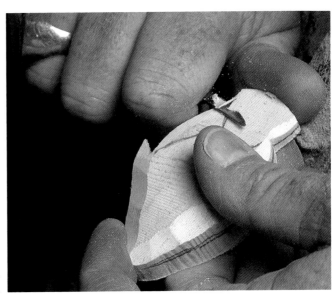

Bob uses the knife to thin down the fins, beginning with the tail fin.

When carving the fins, the pencil line outlining them is often removed. Bob reestablishes this line after it is removed, keeping an important reference mark.

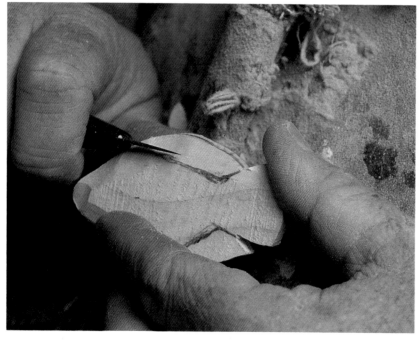

The dorsal fin is carved in a two-step process. First, Bob cuts along the pencil line, keeping the knife blade almost perpendicular with the plane of the fin.

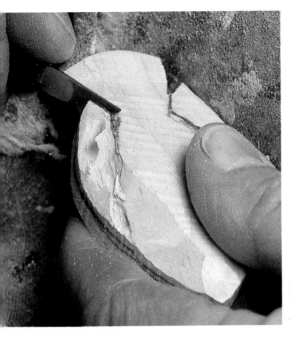

Bob then removes wood along the fin, working back to the line he cut in the previous step.

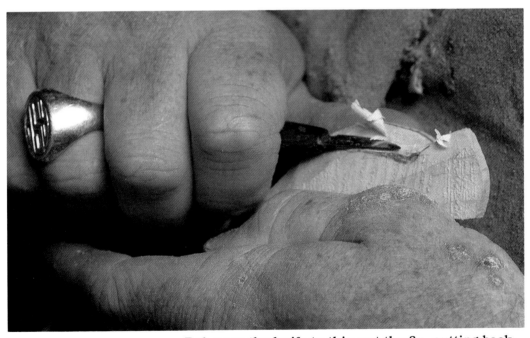

Bob uses the knife to thin out the fin, cutting back to the centerline, thus ensuring that the fin will appear to be in the center of the fish.

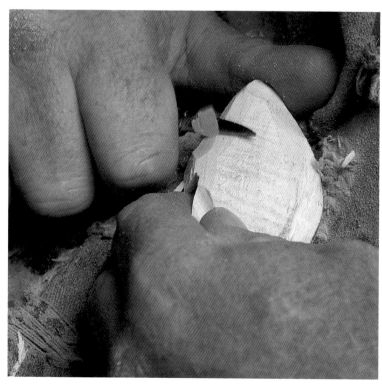

The knife is used to round off the edges of the fish.

A carpenter's rasp is then used to remove knife marks and to further round off the fish and thin down the dorsal fin.

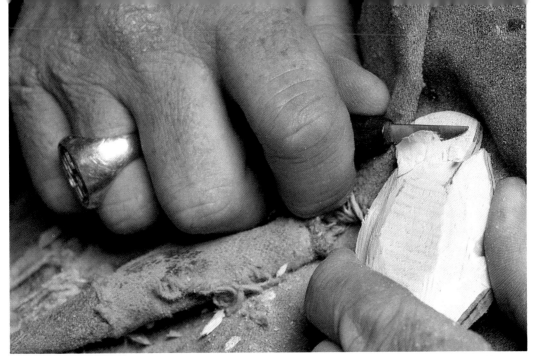

Bob carves the tail fin in the same manner as the dorsal, although he will have this fin angled slightly to the left, providing the illusion of motion. "You don't have to have much of an angle," he says. "All you need is just a suggestion."

The tail fin is tapered with the rasp, emphasizing the contour Bob carved with the knife.

The rasp is used to further round off and smooth
the fish.

The dorsal fin is outlined again with pencil.

Bob uses the small knife to
cut the notch that separates the
dorsal and tail fins.

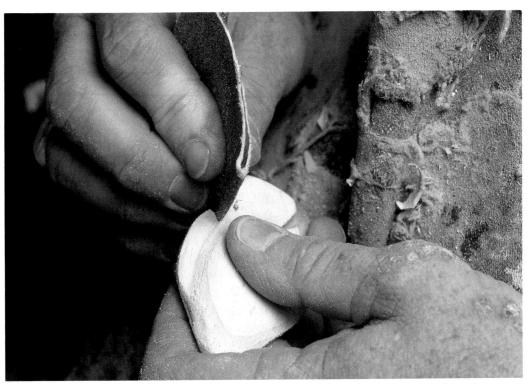

With the general shape of the fish established, Bob
sands the surface to remove rasp marks and to further round off the edges.

The pencil is used to sketch various details. Here Bob draws the line where the rays of the tail fin join the body of the fish.

The gill covers are drawn, using photographs of the fish as reference.

The location of the eyes is also sketched in. Care must be taken in this step to ensure that the eyes are symmetrical. Bob looks at the fish from the front and from the top to make sure that one eye is not higher or lower than the other.

The gill plates are carved in the same manner as the fins. Here Bob cuts along the pencil line perpendicular to the plane of the body.

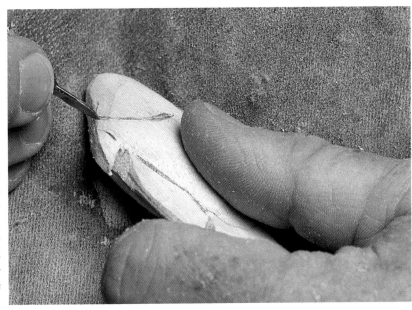

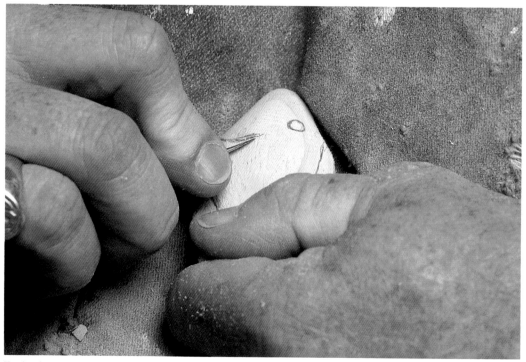

Bob then cuts back to the perpendicular line at an angle of about 30 degrees. This step defines the shape of the gill plates, but the cut does not have to be deep.

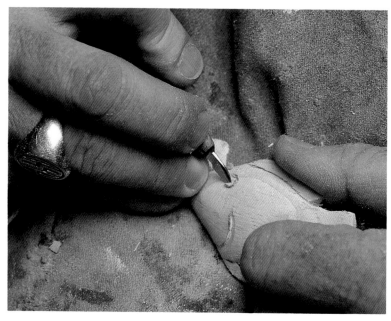

Bob carves the eyes by first cutting around the penciled circle, and then carving back from the center of the eye toward the perimeter. This gives the eye a rounded appearance.

The final step in detailing the fish is to carve the rays of the fins, which Bob does by cutting parallel lines with the knife, using the pencil line as a reference mark.

A notch is carved to represent the mouth, and now the cherubfish is ready for paint.

Bob has carved four fish, which will be mounted and displayed together. Before he begins painting he test-fits the four. The fish are connected by small dowels.

Bob arranges the fish so that they overlap each other, and they are in a C-curve composition, which is more pleasing visually than if the fish were on the same vertical plane. With the arrangement completed, Bob will disassemble it and paint each fish separately, then put it back together.

Bob uses paint thinner to stress the surface of the wood. The fish is held by a brad clamped in Vice-Grip pliers, and the thinner is applied with a brush.

Bob burns off the paint thinner, a step that darkens the wood, seals the pores, and removes "fuzz." This could be a dangerous step, and we don't recommend it. Chemical aging can be done using vinegar and other substances.

The fire burns briefly; then Bob burnishes the fish
with a well-worn bristle brush.

The cherub is now primed,
sealed, and ready for its
first application of color.

Bob uses Ronan brand Japan colors, which are highly saturated oil paints. For this project he will use four colors: chrome yellow light, liberty red medium, Prussian blue, and Van Dyke brown.

Bob mixes yellow and red to create an orange color that is applied to the cheeks of the cherubfish. He purposely does not mix the paint thoroughly in order to create an irregular quality, with red dominating in some areas and yellow in others.

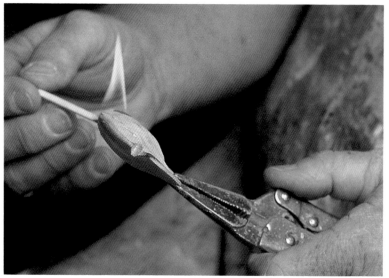

While the orange paint is still wet, Bob burns it. The heat ages the paint and also dries it, allowing him to apply the next color immediately. Again, we do not recommend the use of fire, which has obvious dangers.

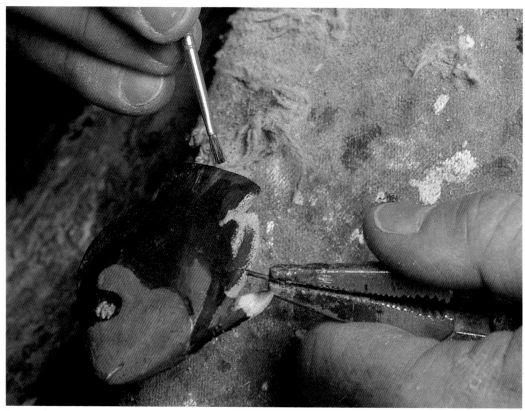

Prussian blue is used to paint the body of the fish. Bob purposely applies the paint unevenly. This will give the fish a slightly worn, folk art quality.

Van Dyke brown is applied to the fins. This will darken them and give them a warm quality, a departure from the coolness of the blue.

Liberty red medium is applied to the eyes.

As a final step, Bob again burns the paint, and then brushes it with a stiff bristle brush. The combination of fire and brushing creates the illusion of age, giving the fish a folk art look.

When all four fish are painted, Bob reassembles the composition. If needed, he touches up the paint where the fish are held together by the wooden dowels. The composition is mounted on a piece of weathered wood.

About the Author

Curtis Badger has written widely about fish and wildfowl art, wildfowl hunting, and conservation issues in general. His articles have appeared in many national and regional magazines, and he has served as editor of *Wildfowl Art Journal*, which is published by the Ward Foundation. He is the co-author of *Painting Waterfowl with J. D. Sprankle*, *Making Decoys the Century-Old Way*, and *Barrier Islands* and the author of *Salt Tide*. He lives in Onancock, Virginia.

The Bird Carving Basics Series
by Curtis J. Badger

This series offers world-class carving tips at a reasonable price. Each volume presents a variety of techniques from carvers like Jim Sprankle, Leo Osborne, Martin Gates, and Floyd Scholz. Illustrated with exceptional step-by-step photos.

The eleven-volume series:

Eyes

Feet

Habitat

Tools

Heads

Bills and Beaks

Texturing

Painting

Special Painting Techniques

Songbird Painting

How to Compete

For complete ordering information, write:
Stackpole Books
5067 Ritter Road
Mechanicsburg, PA 17055
or call 1-800-732-3669